W9-CBU-704

TO

myself, son & daughter

FROM

mom

DATE

Dec. 2011

PHIL CALLAWAY
Photography by KEVIN RIVOLI

Making Life Rich Without Any Money

HARVEST HOUSE PUBLISHERS
EUGENE, OREGON

Cover and interior design by Koechel Peterson and Associates, Minneapolis, Minnesota

Unless otherwise indicated, all Scripture quotations are taken from the Holy Bible, New International Version®, NIV®. Copyright © 1973, 1978, 1984 by Biblica, Inc. ™ Used by permission of Zondervan. All rights reserved worldwide.

Verses marked NLT are taken from the *Holy Bible,* New Living Translation, copyright ©1996, 2004. Used by permission of Tyndale House Publishers, Inc., Wheaton, IL 60189 USA. All rights reserved.

All photos © Kevin Rivoli

Select text is adapted from *Making Life Rich Without Any Money* © 2009 by Phil Callaway. Used by permission.
For more information about Phil Callaway visit www.laughagain.org

MAKING LIFE RICH WITHOUT ANY MONEY GIFT EDITION

Published by Harvest House Publishers

Eugene, Oregon 97402

www.harvesthousepublishers.com

ISBN 978-0-7369-2661-4

All rights reserved. No part of this publication may be reproduced, stored in a retrieval system, or transmitted in any form or by any means—electronic, mechanical, digital, photocopy, recording, or any other—except for brief quotations in printed reviews, without the prior permission of the publisher.

Printed in China

11 12 13 14 15 16 17 18 19 / FC / 10 9 8 7 6 5 4 3 2 1

TABLE OF CONTENTS

*The wealth of man is the number of things which he
loves and blesses, which he is loved and blessed by.*

THOMAS CARLYLE

What Makes Life Rich?

> *Money has never yet made anyone rich.*
>
> LUCIUS ANNAEUS SENECA

Something marvelous took place on the Callaway family tree one December: My parents celebrated their fifty-fifth wedding anniversary. As you know, a fifty-fifth anniversary is as rare these days as checkered zebras, so we blew up balloons, bought gifts, combed the grandkids' hair, and ordered pizza. When the festivities died down, we thought we'd better do something a little out of the ordinary, so we bought space in a city newspaper and placed these words beside a picture of the well-weathered couple:

Happy 55th Wedding Anniversary! From the 5 of us awaiting our inheritance.

When my older brother (a Baptist minister) delivered the ad to the paper, the lady in charge of the classifieds took a long look at it, exhaled slowly, and then asked quite seriously, "You sure you wanna say this? Won't it start a family feud or something?"

She had a good point. After all, baby boomers stand to inherit trillions of dollars over the next couple of decades. But we Callaway kids won't have much to fight over. Our parents spent their entire lives below what the government calls "the poverty line."

I wasn't always thankful for this.

As a five-year-old, I stood before the sink, two pennies in hand, and discovered to my surprise that by simply holding the coins in front of a mirror I could double my assets. *If only I could make money this quickly,* I thought, and then I prayed out loud, "God, please make me rich."

But God didn't seem to hear.

In those days, my father's monthly income was $230—hardly enough to buy sugar for my cereal. As a result, we had no television. No skateboards. No insurance. In fact, we couldn't even afford a phone. One night I overheard Dad say to Mom, "Honey, we have enough money to last us the rest of our lives—unless we live past Thursday."

Thursday came and went, and the years slipped by. Then, ever so slowly, it began to dawn on me that my prayer was being answered. Not in the way I hoped it would be, but in a far better way. At the age of 14, I still hadn't smelled the inside of a new car, savored a Big Mac, or slipped on a brand-new pair of jeans. But I had a backyard to run in, friends to play with, parents who loved me, and the sneaking suspicion that God loved me too.

As a young boy I thought I knew what would make me rich. As a middle-aged man, I'm asking questions of myself and others, rich and poor, old and young, famous and not so famous. What constitutes a truly rich life? How do we leave a lasting legacy? If money isn't enough, what is? And what really matters in the end?

I can't wait to share with you what I've discovered.

THERE IS NO WEALTH BUT LIFE.

JOHN RUSKIN

Top Ten Free (or Almost Free) Things to Do on a First Date

- Pack two lunches in a backpack and go for a trail walk to a vista view.
- Go for a ride on a tandem bike and take turns leading.
- Cook something new and exciting, like fresh salsa or homemade ice cream, or a family favorite.
- Do a walking tour of local art galleries.
- Create a list of fun "get to know you" questions and take turns asking them.
- Go window shopping (or people watching) at the mall.
- Visit a local playground and swing side by side. Share some funny childhood stories.
- Select a free outdoor concert or outdoor showing of a movie and take lots of snacks.
- Set up a treasure hunt to lead your friend to some of your favorite locations around town. Have the last clue lead to a fun dessert place.
- Attend a free lecture at a university or other venue that relates to something you are both interested in.

If the principles of contentment are not within us, the height of station and worldly grandeur will as soon add a cubit to a man's stature as to his happiness.

LAURENCE STERNE

Happiness is dependent on the taste, and not on things. It is by having what we like that we are made happy, not by having what others think desirable.

FRANCOIS VI, DUC DE LA ROCHEFOUCAULD

God has two dwellings: one in heaven, and the other in a meek and thankful heart.

IZAAK WALTON

Simplicity Makes Life Rich

*No man can tell
whether he is rich or
poor by turning to
his wallet.
It is the heart that
makes a man rich.*

HENRY WARD BEECHER

I started asking people on airplanes, in checkout lines, and online one simple question: "What has made your life rich?" One of them turned on me rather abruptly and said, "When people like you leave me alone!"

Thankfully, most found the question a little more interesting, and a few hundred were good enough to respond. They ranged from bestselling authors to concert pianists to real-estate agents. But regardless of their occupation, many share one thing in common. They are realizing that those who slow down enough to enjoy the simple gifts God gives enrich their lives. Here is a small sampling. I hope you'll enjoy these responses as much as I have.

"One year ago we left our crowded apartment atop seven flights of narrow stairs in overpriced New York for a bigger fixer-upper house of our own in a small town. Even with our best calculations, we wondered how it would work. I quit my job. My husband took a pay cut. And we were worried. But our lives are enriched in so many ways. I just learned that twins are on the way. Our priorities have changed. Before, we kept promising ourselves that the next month, things would change. They never did—until we changed them. Our investment in a simpler life is paying off."

"I am a homemaker with two small children and one husband. In the last year I have learned to look positively on the smallest tasks. When I unload the dishwasher, I think of those who will eat off the forks. When I unload the dryer, I sometimes hug the warm clothes and pray for those who will wear them."

"The thing that's made my life rich is the same thing that's kept me most without money: my children (we just had number seven). With kids you experience the full range of emotions: joy, elation, sadness, anger, happiness, sorrow, laughter, tears. You name it, kids will help you experience it. I wouldn't trade a minute with my kids for anything life could have given me without them."

Wondrous is the strength of cheerfulness, and its power of endurance— the cheerful man will do more in the same time and will do it better, will preserve it longer, than the sad or sullen.
THOMAS CARLYLE

Choose such pleasures as recreate much and cost little.
THOMAS FULLER

"I recently rediscovered the Sabbath. Now, instead of shopping, fixing the car, or cleaning the house, our family attends an early church service then spends the day together. We have hiked into the Rocky Mountains, singing at the top of our lungs. We have serenaded the patrons of old folks' homes. And we have sat under pine trees, reading the classics together. Always we are better prepared for Monday because of Sunday."

"Last week I dropped my BlackBerry and watched it shatter into a zillion pieces. For the next few hours I actually had time to play Ping-Pong with my teenage boys, read with my preteen daughter, and spend an hour in the kitchen watching and admiring my wife while carrying on a conversation. Imagine that! Every day now I am taking time for family and shutting off the new phone."

"My father taught me how to fish when I was very young. The fun of catching a big one has never left me, but I'm equally excited to watch my kids or one of their friends reel one in. My dad died this past year, and my son graduated from high school. For his graduation present, we spent a week together fishing in Minnesota. The last night, when we were bringing in the boat, the weather was perfect and the scenery was beautiful. I was pretty emotional, knowing he was on his way to university and this may never happen again. But I also knew that just like me, he would never forget fishing with his dad."

Top Ten Free Ways to Be a Good Friend

- Create a *Book of Thanksgiving*: In a pretty journal, record all the reasons you love your friend.
- Post a note of encouragement on a friend's Facebook page.
- Invite friends over for a themed dinner based on movies, countries, or any other topic. Have each person bring a potluck item related to the theme.
- Do something helpful for your friend anonymously.
- Send an "I'm thinking of you" text message when you know your friend faces a hard day.
- Take a road trip to see a friend you've been missing. Or plan to meet halfway.
- Ask how your friend is doing and plan to spend time really finding out.
- Help a friend with housework… vacuuming, dusting, cleaning windows. It's more fun with two!
- Write and mail a fun or encouraging letter to your friend. Real mail is such a treat.
- Donate to a cause or organization that is meaningful to your friend.

Happiness is like a butterfly which, when pursued, is always beyond our grasp, but, if you will sit down quietly, may alight upon you.

NATHANIEL HAWTHORNE

Often and often to me, and instinctively, has an innocent pleasure felt like a foretaste of infinite delight, an antepast of heaven. Nor can I believe otherwise than that pure happiness is of a purifying effect; like the Jewish bread from heaven, no doubt, it is meant to invigorate as well as to gratify.

WILLIAM MOUNTFORD

Every time a man smiles, and much more when he laughs, it adds something to his fragment of life.

LAURENCE STERNE

It is not how much we have, but how much we enjoy, that makes happiness.

CHARLES SPURGEON

True happiness renders men kind and sensible; and that happiness is always shared with others.

CHARLES DE SECONDAT
MONTESQUIEU

Our brightest blazes of gladness are commonly kindled by unexpected sparks.

SAMUEL JOHNSON

Family Makes Life Rich

We are shaped and fashioned by what we love.

JOHANN WOLFGANG
VAN GOETHE

One morning the phone rang. It was the president of a successful California corporation asking me to consider a prestigious position in his firm. The starting salary? Three times what I was making at the time.

It didn't take long for a smile to cross my face. "Wouldn't it be nice to have a little extra money?" I told my wife, Ramona. "You could use a new wardrobe, and I'd love to buy some of the things I've always wanted, like a car that won't quit and a house that won't leak."

Two weeks later we were on our way to California for a formal interview.

Oak boardrooms have always intimidated me, but this time I felt right at home. This was where I belonged. My sights were set on a bigger house. A newer car. Security. Success.

During the interview, I was intrigued by all that the job offered, including a chance to travel. "How many days a month will I be on the road?" I asked.

There was an uncomfortable silence.

The president looked at me as if he didn't understand the question. Finally he said, "The question isn't how much you'll be gone, Phil. It's how much you'll be home. And it won't be much."

Ramona was nudging me under the table, a wrinkled expression on her face. And later that day on the flight home she expressed her concern. "You have a young family, Phil . . . we'd really like to see you occasionally. . . "

But during our layover in Seattle, I renewed my determination to take the job. As I walked to a nearby restroom, I practiced my acceptance speech.

Entering a tiny stall, I latched the door behind me. Suddenly the place began to shake. Lights flickered and walls shook. For the first time in my life, I was in an earthquake. Now, I don't know if you've thought much about where you would most like to die, but if you're anything like me, your list does not include an airport washroom.

There is a magic in that little word, home; it is a mystic circle that surrounds comforts and virtues never known beyond its hallowed limits.

ROBERT SOUTHEY

He enjoys much who is thankful for little; a grateful mind is both a great and a happy mind.

WILLIAM SECKER

During the next few seconds, brief memories flashed before me: the miraculous birth of our first child. Faces of friends and family. My wife. My kids. There was not one image of a car, a home, or a bulging bank account.

When the rattling stopped, I fled the room. Grabbing my wife I thought, *I'll kiss her and let her feel the earth move one more time.*

Later we learned that the quake had registered 5.0 on Mr. Richter's scale. Believe me, it registered much higher on mine.

On the flight home, I scribbled these words on an airplane napkin:

I will consider myself a success when I am walking close to Jesus every day. When I am building a strong marriage, loving my kids, and performing meaningful work. I will consider myself a success when I'm making others homesick for heaven.

"I'll call California," I told Ramona, taking her hand. And she knew from the smile on my face what I planned to say.

*Home, the spot of earth supremely blest,
a dearer, sweeter spot than all the rest.*

Robert Montgomery

Giving Makes Life Rich

He is richest who is content with the least.

SOCRATES

Your actions, in passing, pass not away, for every good work is a grain of seed for eternal life.

SAINT BERNARD

When I was about five, I found a quarter on a sidewalk one morning (I probably made more than my dad that day!), and before rushing to the candy store, I ran home to show it to my mother. "I'm gonna look for money everywhere I go now," I told her, gasping for breath. My wise mother sat me down and told me a story about a man who found a five-dollar bill in a gutter and spent the rest of his life looking for more. According to my mother, he never saw the trees. He never saw the flowers. He never saw the birds. In fact, he missed a hundred rainbows and a thousand sunsets. All he saw was gutters. "I hope you enjoy that candy, Philip," she said, "but remember . . . always look a little higher."

Here are the stories of some who have learned the joy of looking a little higher. Who are learning what a buck can—and cannot—buy.

"A few years ago our church sent a container of clothes to the Ukraine. We had a hundred dollars that we wanted to spend, so we found a store that would give us a good deal on a hundred dollars' worth of wool work socks. Giving money away has made my life richer."

"We're moving across town to the wrong side of the tracks this week. We're venturing into the Somali slums here in Nairobi. These past two years our lives have been richer because of these refugees. We have fed, clothed, and prayed with people who suffer daily more than I ever thought possible. I've discovered that life is harder than I'd ever imagined, but I have also discovered that God is bigger and better than I'd ever imagined."

"A year ago we decided to quit eating out so much and use the money to support a needy child in Latin America through Compassion International. We keep her picture in our dining room now and pray for her almost every night. Our daughters write her letters and consider her a part of our extended family. It's tough not to feel rich when you're giving money away."

Write your name in kindness, love, and mercy on the hearts of thousands you come in contact with year by year, and you will never be forgotten. Your name and your good deeds will shine as the stars of heaven.

THOMAS CHALMERS

"I noticed the other day that a widow in our town is working two jobs to make ends meet. As an author and speaker, I'm able to make some extra money, so we've started sending her what we can. She doesn't know about it, but our kids sure do. It's probably the only family secret we have. Every time I come back from speaking, the kids want to know . . . can we give more money to our widow friend?"

"A few days after our daughter Jill was born, my wife and I were carrying her out of the hospital to take her home. An elderly man from our church was pacing the lobby. His wife was in the hospital dying of cancer, and he spent most of his time with her.

"Walking up to us with a tired smile, he pressed a 20 dollar bill into my hand. 'My wife and I were never able to have children,' he said. 'But we hear you'll be needing lots of this. God bless you.' Four years have passed, and he is a widower now. Whenever we see him sitting alone at church, our family sits beside him. I'm sure our kids are a little noisy sometimes, but he doesn't seem to mind. And one of them has even started calling him Grandpa. She's his favorite.

"She's our four-year-old, Jill."

Top Ten Things to Do with a Free Weekend

- Load up the car and head for the coast or the mountains.
- Check out your city's local activities guide and do something you haven't done before.
- In the fall, take a day to collect beautiful leaves to press.
- Go to your local visitor information center and become a tourist in your own town for a weekend.
- Tackle a home project that you've been meaning to get to or always wanted to try.
- Rent a weekend's worth of films and have your own movie marathon.
- Hold a horseshoes or croquet tournament for your friends or neighbors.
- Invite a friend over to prepare a new recipe or whole menu—a complicated one that takes a lot of time—and enjoy a leisurely meal together.
- Host a talent night for friends or family. Make it fun with a stage area and applause signs.
- Invite another family over for a weekend campout—indoors or out. Make s'mores, go on a scavenger hunt, work on a gigantic jigsaw puzzle, or take a "hike" through your neighborhood and identify the birds and flowers.

Life is made up, not of great sacrifices or duties, but of little things, in which smiles, and kindnesses, and small obligations, given habitually, are what win and preserve the heart and secure comfort.

SIR HUMPHRY DAVY

LOVE GIVES ITSELF; IT IS NOT BOUGHT.

HENRY WADSWORTH LONGFELLOW

The desire to be beloved is ever restless and unsatisfied; but the love that flows out upon others is a perpetual well-spring from on high.

LYDIA MARIE CHILD

Do all the good you can, in all the ways you can, to all the souls you can, in every place you can, at all the times you can, with all the zeal you can, as long as ever you can.

JOHN WESLEY

Any one reflecting upon the thought he has of the delight, which any present or absent thing is apt to produce in him, has the idea we call love.

JOHN LOCKE

Where there is room in the heart there is always room in the house.

THOMAS MOORE

Gratitude Makes Life Rich

Circumstances and situations do color life, but you have been given the mind to choose what the color shall be.

JOHN HOMER MILLER

This past winter, thanks to a mischievous weatherman and an unending snowfall, we did something a little unusual at our house. After two weeks of brutally cold temperatures and the prognosis of more to come, we decided to brighten the winter blues with a trip to our town's indoor swimming pool. After pumping ourselves up with excitement, however, we were a little deflated to discover that the car wouldn't start. My eldest son was so mad he wanted to set it on fire (something that would have given us all a degree of satisfaction).

Instead I herded the troops back inside and told them I had something else in mind. Something special. "You sit here and watch," I said, "and see if you can guess what it is." Grabbing a shovel, I propped a ladder against the house and climbed onto our gently sloping roof. The kids watched in awe as the heaviest snowfall in history fell past our kitchen window.

Soon, I'd shoveled a six-foot pile of snow into the backyard. Before long, we were having the time of our lives jumping off the roof into what looked like a giant homemade marshmallow. We hollered. We shouted. We threw snowballs. We pretended we were skydivers and stuntmen. We even pretended we were warm.

And afterward, sitting around a heat vent and drinking hot chocolate thick with marshmallows, we all agreed: We were grateful that the car didn't start up because Plan B was so much better than Plan A. "I like winter best of all," said Rachael. "We never drink hot chocolate in the summer."

Our home joys are the most delightful earth affords, and the joy of parents in their children is the most holy joy of humanity. It makes their hearts pure and good.

JOHANN PESTALOZZI

Blessed be the hand that prepares a pleasure for a child,
for there is no saying when and where it may bloom forth.

DOUGLAS JERROLD

NATURE WAS HERE A SERIES OF WONDERS, AND A FUND OF DELIGHT.

DANIEL BOONE

Let us be grateful to people who make us happy; they are the charming gardeners who make our souls blossom.

MARCEL PROUST

Best of all is it to preserve everything in a pure, still heart, and let there be for every pulse a thanksgiving, and for every breath a song.

KONRAD VON GESNER

Friends Make Life Rich

The great use of life is to spend it for something that will outlast it.

WILLIAM JAMES

Friendships are a lot like money. They're easier made than kept. Many people tell me that friendships have made their lives rich. Yet many of those same people wish those friendships were better.

So how can you be a better friend? Here are secrets to great friendships.

1. Accept others. Very few people would tell you, "You know, I haven't been condemned, belittled, or criticized quite enough lately. Go ahead. Hit me with something awful." Each of us longs to be encouraged, built up, and accepted by others. Good friends know that. Good friends accept people the way they are. They appreciate and praise the uniqueness of others. And they allow their friends the freedom to be themselves.

2. Listen up. An old Spanish proverb says, "Two great talkers will not travel far together." How true. To ask questions and stick around for the answers is a noble—maybe even angelic—trait. I have done this twice in my life and have found it powerful and magnetic on both occasions. The ability to show genuine interest in others is an admirable quality of a true friend. When people listen to us, we expand and grow.

3. Keep secrets. Proverbs 20:19 says, "A gossip betrays a confidence; so avoid a man who talks too much." Real friends speak well of you behind your back. They are known as people who won't receive gossip, nor will they pass it on. Remember, a closed mouth gathers no foot. Good friends aren't there just to listen to our secrets; they keep them.

4. Sharpen up. Proverbs 27:17 tells us that we are to sharpen each other "as iron sharpens iron." Years ago a good friend of mine took me out for pie and coffee. "Phil, it's not fun for me to tell you this, but I've felt I needed to confront you about something." I set my fork down and listened. "Sometimes you have a real problem with gossip."

I was steamed. Offended. I sat there eating pie, thinking of his problems. But the more I thought about his words, the more I realized he was right on the money. Today, though we are many miles apart, I consider him to be one of my truest friends.

The language of friendship is not words but meanings.
HENRY DAVID THOREAU

Friendship is precious, not only in the shade, but in the sunshine of life, and thanks to a benevolent arrangement the greater part of life is sunshine.

THOMAS JEFFERSON

5. Practice forgiveness. When a friend who works in an office near mine came to work one morning, he found a can of Coke on his desk. On the side was a Post-it note bearing these words: "Sorry. I was a jerk. Will you ever forgive me?" Smiling, he walked down the hall with a message of forgiveness. You may have already guessed. The writer of the note was me. And later that day my friend brought me a can of Pepsi.

Good friends humble themselves enough to admit when they are wrong. And good friends forgive. In fact, the gift of forgiveness is often the best gift we can offer a friend. And if it is accompanied by a can of soda, so much the better.

6. Focus upward. An old Turkish proverb goes like this: "He who seeks a faultless friend is friendless." How true. Friends fail. People disappoint. Realizing that the very best friends on earth will disappoint us takes the pressure off our friendships and strengthens them. God does not promise that *people* will never leave us or forsake us. He promises that *he* will never leave.

7. Be there. There's nothing like sickness or bankruptcy to help us discover who our real friends are. During a time when my wife was ill, her friend Julie informed us that she would be babysitting our three kids each Wednesday afternoon. And so each week, Julie would show up and "kidnap" the kids, much to my wife's delight. To this day, Ramona often comments about Julie's kindness. When possible, be there when a friend needs you. If you can't be there, send a note or make a phone call.

Friendships that last a lifetime require nurturing, kindness, and a listening ear. Those who make such an investment find it pays off all through the years.

Top Ten Ways to Freely Give

- Donate clothing, food, housewares, and toiletries to a local shelter.
- Volunteer at an elementary school or library to help children learn to read.
- Brainstorm how your personal gifts could be put to use in your church, community, and neighborhood…and use them!
- Write letters of encouragement to soldiers, friends you never see, teachers, pastors, and others in leadership.
- Bake a loaf of bread or some cookies for your neighbor, just because.
- Volunteer at a local animal shelter. This is perfect for teaching kids to give and to be kind to animals.
- Offer to read books or letters to residents at a nursing home once a month.
- Babysit for a single parent or a family so they can have a free night out.
- Instead of having a garage sale, have a garage giveaway! Make space in your home and pass along useful items to others.
- Locate a community garden that helps feed those in need and volunteer some green-thumb time.

I have friends in overalls whose friendship I would not swap for the favor of the kings of the world.

THOMAS EDISON

If instead of a gem, or even a flower, we should cast the gift of a loving thought into the heart of a friend, that would be giving as the angels give.

GEORGE MACDONALD

*Nothing but heaven itself is better
than a friend who is really a friend.*

PLAUTUS

There is nothing on this earth more to be prized than true friendship.

SAINT THOMAS AQUINAS

*There is one friend in
the life of each of us who
seems not a separate
person, however dear and
beloved, but an expansion,
an interpretation, of one's
self, the very meaning of
one's soul.*

EDITH WHARTON

Faith Makes Life Rich

*The soul is strong
that trusts in
goodness.*
MASSINGER

B y summer we had seen 21 specialists, scoured libraries for literature, and tried to diagnose my wife's mystery illness ourselves. Still her seizures continued.

Every night we lay awake in the darkness, unable to sleep. And sometimes panic overtook me. "What do I do now, Lord? Where do we go from here?" There was only silence. The windows of heaven seemed to be shut, the shutters drawn tight.

Then verses my mother had drummed into me when I was a child came back to comfort us. "God is our refuge and strength, an ever-present help in trouble. Therefore we will not fear, though the earth give way and the mountains fall into the heart of the sea" (Psalm 146:1-3). "'For I know the plans I have for you,' declares the LORD, 'plans to prosper you and not to harm you, plans to give you hope and a future'" (Jeremiah 29:11).

But even hope seemed to be slipping from our grasp. The seizures worsened, occurring every day and sometimes every half hour. I rarely left Ramona's side, and late one night, after she was finally asleep, I paced our darkened backyard and fell to my knees pounding the ground. "God," I cried, "I can't take it anymore. Please do something."

I would love to tell you that I saw handwriting in the sky or heard an audible voice. But instead, as I stood to my feet, a doctor's name came to mind. We attended the same church, but I'd never thought to ask Dan his opinion. Minutes later I had him on the phone. After listening to my description, he said simply, "I think I can help. Bring her to see me first thing in the morning."

Sure enough. Dan prescribed a simple antiseizure medication all the other doctors had overlooked.

Faith is the substance of things hoped for, the evidence of things not seen.

THE BOOK OF HEBREWS

I've learned from experience that the great part of our happiness or misery depends on our dispositions and not on our circumstances.

MARTHA WASHINGTON

I don't know if I really believed in miracles before that point in my life. But within a week, Ramona was a different person. Her eyes lit up with the sparkle that first attracted me to her. The seizures ended. God had given my wife back to me.

Of course, we're not home yet. More tests are ahead. But every day my wife wakes up beside the most thankful guy in the world. I'm thankful that God's grace *does* accompany life's surprises. That in the toughest of times, his grace can help us choose joy over bitterness and help us stay together when our whole world is falling apart.

Top Ten Ways to Be Free from Worry

- Do something creative: paint, write, play an instrument, or knit.
- Pray for others and then find a way to help them in your own way.
- Watch an action-packed movie.
- Talk to people you trust…and listen to their advice about not worrying.
- Spend 15 minutes a day in your garden or sitting outside to appreciate nature's beauty.
- Start a "thankfulness" journal and record everything you're thankful for. Read it often!
- Exercise! Even a 15-minute walk outside can clear your head and boost your health.
- Take a long nap or bath (or both!) and allow yourself the restoration time you need.
- Put on your favorite music and dance as you belt out the tunes.
- Work up a personal mission statement and goals, and then stick to them.

God be praised, who, to believing souls, gives light in darkness, comfort in despair.

WILLIAM SHAKESPEARE

Hope is the best part of our riches. What sufficeth it that we have the wealth of the Indies in our pockets, if we have not the hope of heaven in our souls?

CHRISTIAN NESTELL BOVEE

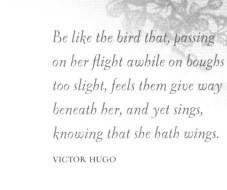

Be like the bird that, passing
on her flight awhile on boughs
too slight, feels them give way
beneath her, and yet sings,
knowing that she hath wings.

VICTOR HUGO

Be not afraid of life. Believe that
life is worth living and your belief
will help create the fact.

WILLIAM JAMES

There is no medicine like hope,
no incentive so great, and no
tonic so powerful as expectation of
something tomorrow.

ORISON SWETT MARDEN

*In actual life every great enterprise begins
with and takes its first forward step in faith.*

AUGUST WILHELM VON SCHLEGEL

Joy and Laughter Make Life Rich

Let a joy keep you. Reach out your hands and take it when it runs by.

CARL SANDBURG

Spring is snowball season where I live. The warm west winds descend from the mountains to turn drifts into slush and adults into children. The other day on my way to work I was hit between the shoulder blades with a hard-packed ball of ice. Ouch. Turning around, I saw the culprit. A five-year-old with one hand clasped over her mouth. Perhaps she didn't think her aim was that good. I was in a hurry. Deadlines to meet. Phone calls to make. But for some reason, I bent down and fashioned a few weapons of my own. And for the next few minutes we engaged in a delightful battle. A battle which I lost. Quite badly.

Later the little girl's mother came to my office. She was a single mom. She'd had a tough day. The job she applied for didn't pan out. The car she needed, she couldn't afford. But for a minute or two a snowball fight had helped lighten her load. "I want to thank you," she said with tears in her eyes.

When we leave this earth, we won't take much. The U-Haul doesn't follow the hearse, they say. But I'm glad that we can leave a few things behind. We can leave footprints everywhere we go. Grace-full footprints. Footprints of encouragement. Of kindness. Of forgiveness. Of love. Of joy and laughter. Footprints that others will want to follow.

* * *

The other day I asked my 11-year-old son, Stephen, "If you had your life to live over again, what would you do differently?" Before he knew I was kidding, he answered, "Eat more candy."

All work and no rest takes the spring and bound out of the most vigorous life. Time spent in judicious resting is not time wasted, but time gained.

M.B. GRIER

I still find each day too short for all the thoughts I want to think, all the walks I want to take, all the books I want to read, and all the friends I want to see.

JOHN BURROUGHS

I laughed at first, but the more I thought about his words, the more I realized the wisdom in them.

You see, I'm one of those people who lives life sensibly hour after hour, day after day. Sometimes I wonder where I got the notion that God is only pleased with my work. In the same way that I love to watch my children chase one another down a sandy beach, so God is pleased when we go barefoot. In the same way that I cheer when my daughter sinks a basketball (yes, this has happened), so God is pleased when we play.

When I was a boy, I heard people say that it's better to burn out than to rust out, and I found myself wondering if there wasn't a better alternative. Years later I've noticed that some of those very same people are the most miserable humans I know. In chasing dreams they missed waking up to the simple joys around them.

I haven't arrived yet. I'm still learning to juggle a busy schedule while enjoying the simple gifts God gives. I'm still learning that there is freedom in slowing down and that there are riches in simplicity.

WONDER IS
INVOLUNTARY PRAISE.

OWEN D. YOUNG

Recreation is not being idle; it is easing the wearied part by change of occupation. To re-create strength, rest. To re-create mind, repose. To re-create cheerfulness, hope in God, or change the object of attention to one more elevated and worthy of thought.

EDWARD C. SIMMONS

Contentment opens the source of every joy.

JAMES BEATTIE

15 Ways to Add Joy to Your Life

1. As often as you can, give thanks.
2. Reread a favorite book.
3. If possible, have a pet.
4. Take your child for a walk (if you don't have a child, borrow one from a friend).
5. Refrain from envy. Genuinely compliment those who have more than you.
6. Make Sunday a day of rest. Start by leaving your watch off (especially during the sermon).
7. Learn to say no politely and quickly.
8. Learn more about the stars. Then lie on your back and find them.
9. Wave at children on school buses.
10. Buy a bird feeder and hang it outside your window.
11. Learn to enjoy food. Take longer to eat it.
12. Don't major on minor issues.
13. Don't give your kids the best of everything. Give them your best.
14. Never miss a chance to read a child a story.
15. When you're alone in the car, sing loudly. Don't forget to roll up the windows!

Who is not attracted by bright and pleasant children, to prattle, to creep, and to play with them?

EPICTETUS

He that will make a good use of any part of his life must allow a large part of it to recreation.

JOHN LOCKE

The most delicate, the most sensible of all pleasures, consists in promoting the pleasure of others.

JEAN DE LA BRUYERE

Life must be lived as play.

PLATO